TEA TIME SELF-TALK

A LITTLE AFTERNOON BLISS FOR LIVING YOUR MAGICAL LIFE

KRISTEN HELMSTETTER

Green
Butterfly
Press

ABOUT THE AUTHOR

In 2018, Kristen Helmstetter sold everything to travel the world with her husband and daughter. She currently splits her time between Florida and a medieval hilltop town in Umbria, Italy.

She writes romance novels under the pen name Brisa Starr.

Listen to *Coffee Self-Talk with Kristen Helmstetter* wherever you listen to podcasts.

You can find her on Instagram:

 instagram.com/coffeeselftalk

OTHER BOOKS BY KRISTEN HELMSTETTER

Coffee Self-Talk: 5 Minutes a Day to Start Living Your Magical Life

The Coffee Self-Talk Starter Pages: A Quick Daily Workbook to Jumpstart Your Coffee Self-Talk

The Coffee Self-Talk Daily Readers (#1 & #2): Bite-Sized Nuggets of Magic to Add to Your Morning Routine

Pillow Self-Talk: 5 Minutes Before Bed to Start Living the Life of Your Dreams

Wine Self-Talk: 15 Minutes to Relax & Tap Into Your Inner Genius

The Coffee Self-Talk Guided Journal: Writing Prompts & Inspiration for Living Your Magical Life

Coffee Self-Talk for Dudes: 5 Minutes a Day to Start Living Your Legendary Life

Coffee Self-Talk for Teen Girls: 5 Minutes a Day for Confidence, Achievement & Lifelong Happiness

The Coffee Self-Talk for Teen Girls Guided Journal: Writing Prompts & Inspiration for Girls in High School

To all of my fabulous Coffee Self-Talk fans in the UK who said, "But I drink tea!"

I dedicate this book to you. I love you all so much.

INTRODUCTION

A few years ago, I was not a very happy person. Though I'd been living a life that many people would have considered great, I did not see this greatness, and instead, I woke up each morning feeling like I lived under a dark cloud.

I felt anxiety about so many things. I saw all of my problems as serious threats. I had deep fears. I over-analyzed everything. I constantly wrestled with my emotions. And I was trapped in this mental pattern for decades, but I just figured we all have problems, right? This was life.

But something nagged at me over the years. Something like destiny, or a little fairy trying to whisper in my ear: *Life isn't supposed to feel like this. You're supposed to smile most of the time. We're destined for more fun. Happiness. Joy. Magic, even.*

So I tried different things to make myself feel better, but it wasn't until I discovered how powerful my mind was—and I changed my *self-talk*—that I dramatically changed my life. My dark clouds started to dissipate. The sun started to peek through. Before long, I experienced gloriously sunny days on a regular basis.

This happy, sun-shiny mood became my new normal, and I totally transformed into a new person. All because of my self-talk, that is, the words I say and the thoughts I think about myself, the world, and my life.

But my new, happy mood was only the beginning. With this change in my outlook, I started making bold decisions and taking action and manifesting amazing things in my life, from abundance, to love, all with tons of motivation, and purpose, and direction, and all with an incredible peace of mind as the backdrop to everything I did. If I'd known my self-talk would change my life so dramatically, I would have started decades ago. It's one of those head-shaking, *woulda-shoulda* moments—lol. But better late than never!

In my book, *Coffee Self-Talk*, I tell the story of how I hit on the discovery that changed my life: creating a daily self-talk ritual and combining it with my morning cup of coffee. In that book, I go into depth about how self-talk works, its life-changing benefits, and how to create your own morning ritual with scripts I provide or that you write yourself.

This *Tea Time* book is different. I'll provide just a quick overview of self-talk for those who are new to it, and we'll jump straight into what I call *Tea Time Self-Talk*, short little pre-written, inspirational sessions that are perfect for a 5-minute, afternoon tea break, or any time you'd like a few minutes of bliss to catch your breath, get centered, and appreciate the beauty of your magical life.

As you can imagine, I love my positive self-talk. So, I use this power to program my mind on a regular basis, literally every day. That's *the key*—doing it so regularly that it's automatic, and you do it almost every day. That's what makes the life changes happen fast. It makes all the difference in the world as you train your brain to think differently. When you do this regularly, you change your life. You transform. You find happiness like you've never known before... because *this stuff works*.

I mean, it's great to tell someone to think positively and optimistically. It all sounds fine on paper. But it doesn't help you if you don't actually *do* the thing. *You have to put it into practice.* In fact, you want to make it a *very* regular habit. And the absolute best way to never miss a day is to connect it with some existing routine or activity that you enjoy. The more formal the ritual, the better... like a *ceremony*.

That's why I do my self-talk in the morning, with my coffee, and also at night as I fall asleep (see my other book, *Pillow Self-Talk*).

Well, I found that between 2 and 4 PM, my day had a little lull, and some days I'd find myself yawning. A cup of tea provided the perfect pick-me-up, and I'd usually drink one at my desk, continuing my work. After a couple weeks of this, when I realized that this afternoon tea time had become a new ritual of sorts, I knew I had an opportunity to slap some sassy-good self-talk to it. And so I started dedicating this time officially, as an afternoon ceremony to give me that beautiful little boost of energy (caffeine and words), and to inspire my happiest mindset to finish my tasks and day with a smile.

What Is Tea Time Self-Talk?

Tea Time Self-Talk is a wonderful little ceremony that takes only five minutes a day. It helps you change your life with feelings of inspiration, motivation, and rejuvenation. It helps you attract the life you want to live, the one that burns so strongly in your heart. All this, with your next cup of tea.

Tea Time Self-Talk comprises two things: 1) your tea time, and 2) your self-talk. (If you're not familiar with self-talk—then holy smokes(!) get ready to change your life! More on that in the next chapter.)

Taking a break with tea in the afternoon is not new. There's the popular, quintessential experience of British tea time, which apparently began with Anna, the 7th Duchess of Beford (1788-1861). Anna began the practice of having tea and snacks in the afternoon to stave off hunger until dinner. Those cute sandwiches and the hats—I'm all over that!

I've also always been intrigued by the Japanese tea ceremony, which honors balance, simplicity, and respect. Practitioners prepare their minds for the ceremony by focusing on life's harmony, leaving stress behind, and finding peace of mind. I love that... we could all benefit from it.

So while afternoon tea is not new, what is new is taking your tea time and using it to help you live your magical life by combining it with rich, positive affirmations and beautiful, uplifting thoughts. It's a boost in delightful energy to round out your day (cute, triangular sammiches and fancy hats optional) and creating your magnificent mindset to inspire you. To motivate you. To rejuvenate your soul.

QUICK SIDENOTE: WHAT IS SELF-TALK?

Before we dive into your tea time self-talk ceremony, for those of you who are new to self-talk, here's a brief primer on what self-talk is and why it will freakin' change your life.

If you've already read *Coffee Self-Talk*, where I take you on a deep-dive into the importance of self-talk, then you can skip this part (though if it's been a while, the refresher might be helpful). And if you haven't read *Coffee Self-Talk*, I recommend it, so you, too, get that deep understanding, which will really inspire you to make your self-talk a major focus in your life.

Self-Talk

So... here's the short version: Self-talk is simply the words you say and think to yourself. It's your inner voice, your internal dialog. Sometimes it's spoken, sometimes it's silent. Sometimes you're aware of it, usually you're not... until you are.

You've been using self-talk your whole life. We all do, because it's our thoughts. It's our thoughts about ourselves, and our hair, and our waist lines, and our abilities. It's our thoughts about what we see on TV and social media. It's our opinions and judgments of other people. It's our attitudes about everything in the commentary that's always running in our mind. So we have self-talk every waking hour, 365 days a year.

Your self-talk is the dialog you run in your head about yourself: the way you see yourself in the mirror, the way you think about yourself and the things you do, and the way you see things outside of yourself, such as the world around us.

Do you like your body? Or do you criticize yourself? Do you think you're clever or creative? Or do you think you're ho-hum? Do you think you're lucky, or do you feel like you attract bad circumstances? Do you love life, or fear it? Do you hate things? Do you frequently judge others negatively... or do you always look for the good in others? Do you like you?

That's your self-talk.

The Good, the Bad, and the Ugly

As you can see, self-talk can be good or bad. Or downright ugly. What you need to know is that, if your self-talk is amazing, then you live an amazing life. If it's so-so, you live a mediocre life. And, if your self-talk is crappy and ugly, then you aren't likely to be very happy, or you find yourself struggling.

Your self-talk can either help you or harm you, because everything you say and feel about you and your life *becomes your truth.* You affirm it with your words—positively or negatively. Your mind... your subconscious... believes what you say, whether it's true or not.

The Shocker

Here's the shocking part: Most people have *no idea* how truly harmful their negative self-talk is. And they have no idea how often they're saying and thinking these negative things. When I first started doing this, I took note of how many of my thoughts and utterances were positive, negative, or neutral, and it *blew my mind* how many of them were negative, despite thinking I was generally a positive person.

You want as little of the bad as possible.

It seems so innocent... you trip and stumble, or you drop your phone on the pavement, you forget to wash your kid's football jersey, or forget to pay a bill on time. In these cases, the words that reflexively come out of your mouth aren't usually positive. It's natural to be upset, right? Or you look in the mirror and squinch your face in different directions, wishing for fewer wrinkles or clearer skin, and the resulting thoughts are negative.

Or you send someone a text message, and they don't reply immediately (gasp!), and you start to wonder if they still like you. Or your co-worker comes by with a new haircut and you think, *"Yikes. Well, it'll grow."*

That's all negative self-talk.

Even negative judgments and opinions about others are a reflection of your own mindset. Most people don't realize how many negative thoughts they think, until they learn that every thought is their self-talk, and their self-talk can make or break them.

This doesn't mean you can't dislike things or have preferences. But you want to focus on what you WANT *waaaay* more than what you don't want, because your life experiences are based on your thoughts. The better your self-talk, the better your life will be!

The Bottom Line

Your self-talk determines your focus, and it determines whether you're happy or not, successful or not, and enjoying life... or not. There's never a time when you're not using your self-talk to manifest—good things or bad things—because the words and feelings inside you determine what comes into your life. You attract that which you think about the most.

By taking control over your self-talk, you create new, better beliefs, and you start taking actions that support those beliefs, so you can start living your magical life.

Ok, let's get started!

INSTRUCTIONS

How to Do Tea Time Self-Talk

In *Tea Time Self-Talk*, I share inspiration and motivation about self-talk in a daily tea time format. The purpose is to help you enjoy a few minutes in your afternoon, just for you, infusing your mind with magnificent, magical thinking!

When you're ready for your Tea Time Self-Talk session, grab this book and your cup of delicious tea. Of course, you don't have to drink tea. You can drink kombucha, sparkling water, coffee, decaf, or even Drambuie. Whatever you want.

Have a seat, get comfy, and read one of the daily entries. It's fine to read them out of order. Think about the words you're reading, while sipping on your tea, feeling inspired and rejuvenated. A perfect little boost of positive energy and light in your afternoon, setting up the rest of your day for success and happiness. A lovely, little ceremony designed to rejuvenate you, and make you shine.

The Tea Time Self-Talk Format

Each day contains two pages. On the left-facing page, you'll read something designed to inspire you or make you think.

On the right-facing page, you'll find your Tea Time Self-Talk script of positive affirmations. Read them out loud, if possible, even if it's just a whisper. For maximum effect, read through the script 4 times.

This repetition is very important. For these short scripts, your first and second passes are just getting you warmed up. On the third pass, the meaning starts to sink in. By the fourth pass, you're more likely to start entering a slightly trance-like state, in which your subconscious becomes very receptive.

The increased repetition and time you spend doing this is part of the magical formula to changing your beliefs, elevating your emotions, and helping you draw your dreams to you faster. As I like to think... the more you read it, the stronger it sinks into you and hooks its magical little claws into you.

Create pictures in your mind of what the words mean to you. Feel free to change any words to ones that suit you best. Believe in yourself. And be on your merry way!

Reading affirmations (especially out loud) can feel weird at first, but it gets easier with time. And sometimes it's hard to think of ourselves so positively, at first, when we've spent so much of our lives criticizing ourselves or feeling less than worthy. Well, this book is here to fix that! To get you using better self-talk! So give yourself permission to start speaking and thinking about yourself in brazen, bold, inspiring words that get you amped and raring to live your best life.

In time, you'll come to believe everything you say. You'll see how it helps you manifest your desires.

But you have to show up! Be relentless in the pursuit of your dreams and epic transformation. Believe in yourself. Believe in your dreams. Believe in the *process.*

Because our brains are utterly amazing and making all our dreams come true.

~

Free Bonus PDF

If you'd like to receive a PDF with ten bonus Tea Times, write to me, and be sure to ask for the "Tea Time Goodies":

Kristen@KristenHelmstetter.com

TEA TIME #1

When you take a moment to think of just one awesome thing in your life right now, it creates a blast of brightness in your day, shining light over everything else.

What's awesome right now in your day? Or in your life? Take the next couple of minutes to appreciate it. Let the positive feelings that swirl through you emanate outward. Focusing on awesome things is what makes your whole life more awesome.

Today is my day.

I am the master of my mind.

I am in charge of my emotions.

I choose to be happy.

I choose peace.

I choose to smile.

I am a phenomenal success at everything I undertake today.

TEA TIME #2

Sometimes, a barrier to manifesting is not owning the beautiful feeling of *deserving* it.

Sometimes people feel guilt when they use the words, "I deserve." But this suggests a lack of self-worth. You deserve all of your desires because you are full of love and gratitude. Because you're a kind and deserving person. And your self-talk should reflect this.

So think about something you want in your life, whether it's a new job, or more money, or romance, or a fun vacation, and say right now, "*I deserve* ____." Fill in the blank, and fill your mind with love and gratitude for the thing you want. Imagine yourself having that thing with ease. Feel uplifted. Feel confidence about it coming to you. Are you ready to receive it?

I'm worthy of feeling wonderful and happy.

I'm worthy of having tons of energy.

I'm worthy of generating abundant income.

I'm worthy of giving and receiving love.

I'm worthy of having great friends.

I'm worthy of seeing opportunities around every corner.

I'm worthy! I'm worthy! I'm worthy!

TEA TIME #3

One way to jump-start your life is by asking questions.

And one of my favorite questions is: *Why?*

If something happened recently that confused you, or frustrated you, or excited you... ask yourself, *Why?* Why did it confuse or frustrate you? Or why did it excite you? Why did it happen? When you start asking the right questions in your life, you start to get useful answers. And these answers help direct your actions. These answers inspire you to take new avenues and embark on new adventures.

Think about events from the past week, and ask yourself questions about them, in order to clarify your feelings about the events. See what you discover about yourself in the process.

I believe in my abilities.

I am so happy today!

I am worthy of living a magical life full of pixie dust, rainbows, and shooting stars!

I have fun, and all of my dreams come.

I love asking questions.

The answers to my questions come to me easily.

I love discovering new things about myself.

TEA TIME #4

Are you being true to yourself?

Are you taking time to nourish your soul in the way that feels best to you?

Life needs you to be your most authentic self. You are here for a reason. And the world needs *you to be you*. If you're not living up to your fullest potential, then now is the moment to start. Make a commitment, today, to show up to the world as the *best possible you*. With all of your unique, quirky, and magnificent traits.

What does it mean for you to really be you? Is there something new you can start doing right now? Is there something the real you would stop doing?

Think about it, plan it, and commit to it.

I am meant for great things.

I am here for a reason.

I appreciate me. I appreciate life.

The world appreciates me. I appreciate the world.

I am living up to my fullest potential.

I am worthy of all my commitments.

I am true to myself. I honor me.

TEA TIME #5

Belief plays a huge part in the success of habits taking root. When you believe in something, it fuels your efforts.

When you believe in *you*, it makes you feel like soaring toward your dream life, instead of slogging through quicksand.

Think about a new habit you'd like to start. It could be an exercise habit, or a meditation habit, or a gratitude habit. Ask yourself *why* you want this habit. Next, *believe* that it's a desirable habit. This sounds obvious, but many people think they want to start a habit, but they haven't really thought about how it would improve their life, and they don't follow through.

You want to feel good about your habit. Not just because other people say it's good, but because you believe it yourself. Give your new habit a positive meaning for yourself, and be very clear about its benefits, and this will align your will with your purpose.

What new habit do you want to adopt?

I love learning.

I am adding good habits to my life.

I am worthy of having great habits.

I have purpose.

I make it happen. I show up to my life and do what it takes.

My good habits take root because I believe in them.

I believe in me.

TEA TIME #6

Repetition is a key part of making a new habit take root. Committing to doing your habit for at least 21 days straight is a great formula for making your habit stick.

On day 22, if you stop the habit, your brain notices that you haven't done it. And it feels like something is missing, prompting you to do the habit. Isn't that amazing? Our brains are so cool.

Today, think about a new habit you want to start, and commit to doing it for at least 21 days.

I commit to myself and my life.

I show up to my life, because my life is meaningful.

I am amazing, and I love my life!

I'm having fun, and great habits are fun!

I awaken my own fire inside me. I'm ready.

Great habits fuel my manifesting power.

It's time. I'm ready. Let's go!

TEA TIME #7

When you do, think, or feel something repeatedly, it becomes baked into your mindset. This means your brain gets used to these thoughts and feelings, and they become your default way of thinking and being.

The repetition of going to the gym a few times a week will build stronger muscles. Your brain responds similarly to your repeated thought patterns, beliefs, behaviors, and habits. Your brain gets stronger. What awesome control you have! But with great power comes great responsibility. Training your brain is up to you. It's your responsibility.

New thinking? New you!

What are you going to start thinking positively about that will be a change for you?

I know the power of my mind.

I use the power of my mind wisely.

I make great choices, and my brain listens.

I keep my thoughts happy and healthy, because it means everything.

I have a phenomenal brain.

My thought patterns make me smile.

I am worthy of living a beautiful life.

TEA TIME #8

What does a real best-friend-forever (BFF) do? In other words, what makes a BFF, a BFF?

Make a list (in your mind or on paper) of what you came up with... because, guess what? You're going to become *your own BFF*. How? By doing the things on your list for yourself, because when you do, the magic starts. That's when real transformation begins.

Why? Because you feel supported. Loved. You have more belief in what you want. You feel more confidence.

How are you going to be your own BFF, today and going forward?

I am my own best friend, because I'll be with me the rest of my life.

I'm a great best friend to myself.

My dreams burn bright inside me, and I support my efforts 100%.

I am full of love and appreciation for myself.

Go, me! Go!

I look at myself, into my own face, into my own eyes, down into my own beautiful soul. I am beautiful. I am strong.

TEA TIME #9

Your brain is always listening to everything you say and think. It doesn't have an opinion on the things you say, it just acts upon them.

Think of your subconscious as a lieutenant waiting for your directions. Ready for marching orders, clipboard and pencil in hand. And that direction comes in the form of *every word, thought, and feeling* that goes through you. *You* create a blueprint for your subconscious to manifest.

Do you want that manifestation to be amazing? Then think amazing thoughts. But if you think poor and negative thoughts, your subconscious will go to work manifesting bad things, and that's what you'll see more of in your life.

You really are in control. And your brain just sits there, waiting for directions.

What are you directing your brain to do today?

I am full of love right now.

I love my body just the way I am today.

I am happy, because I can be.

I am generous, because I choose to be.

I always see the good in any situation.

I am worthy of my dreams.

I love me.

TEA TIME #10

Is there something you need to let go of right now?

Is there something big, like a relationship? Or some mistake you made in the past that continues to bother you? Or is there something small you could let go of, like going through your closet and getting rid of the things you haven't worn in a year?

Letting go is a powerful exercise. It serves your soul. It's when we cling to things that we feel stress and tension. The act of grasping, a clenched fist, prevents your hands from being open to receive. Often, when we let go of things that no longer serve us (attitudes, thoughts, physical items), that's when we receive our deepest desires.

So, is there something you need to let go of, right now?

I let go of things that don't serve my life.

It's easy to let things go.

I have peace in my mind.

I am calm in my heart when letting go.

I know what's best for me.

I always have my best interests at heart.

Letting go brings me freedom.

TEA TIME #11

Are there any difficult relationships in your life?

Well, if you're looking for that person to be what *you* want, then you're going about it the wrong way. Gandhi said, *"You need to be the change that you wish to see in the world."* It's true.

You need to be the person to get the relationship on a better track. *You* start the ball rolling in the right direction. And don't give me any *But! But! But! He did this! She did that!*

Yes, this can seem difficult at first. But once you start, it actually feels wonderful. It always feels better to spread love.

Here are some tips: 1) Start by thinking of positive things about the other person, even if it's just one thing. 2) Make the effort, and start the next conversation. 3) Make the effort, and be the first one to smile. 4) Make the effort, and be the first one to say thank you, or to give a compliment.

Are you willing to make the first move, to improve the situation?

I know that my happiness is my responsibility, and nobody else's.

Other people don't control me. I control me.

Happy relationships start with me.

I honor other people, and I see the best in them.

I enjoy looking for the gems in other people.

I am grateful for my relationships All of them.

I love being the first person to get things going. It's part of who I am.

TEA TIME #12

As you enjoy your delicious tea, fill in the following blanks:

I am happy because _____.

I am also happy because _____.

I love _____ because _____.

I am grateful for _____.

I cherish _____.

I love _____.

I appreciate _____ because _____.

I am lucky to have _____.

I am happy.

I am grateful.

I am love.

I am cherished.

I am thankful.

I appreciate.

I am lucky.

TEA TIME #13

Do you ever feel like you have so much to do that you don't even know where to start? Do you frequently feel overwhelmed?

If so, well, it's time to relax. Just take a moment right now, because you can handle it. Remember to find some happy, because living a magical life doesn't require so much tension, nor the feeling of constantly playing defense. It's about enjoying the process and *believing* that you have an abundance of time.

Are you ready to feel abundance and peace about your time and schedule? Bring this feeling of an abundance of time into your mindset right now with this script.

I have an abundance of time to do everything I want.

I have an abundance of energy to meet all of my needs with a smile.

I have an abundance of resources to make my dreams come true.

I am full of energy. I am full of patience. I am full of love.

I am extremely capable.

I have an abundance of time.

I have an abundance of time.

TEA TIME #14

When you work on manifesting your dreams and goals, it's easy to get frustrated with unknowns. But it's important to remember that your dream life might manifest... *in a way you never imagined.*

You might think you know the best path to achieving your goals, but there's a very good chance that your journey will take unpredictable turns, while still delivering you to your desired dream destination. Or someplace even better!

It can be uncomfortable dealing with the unknown. I totally understand. But instead, I want you to think of it as *exciting.* You want to have plans, and keep taking steps toward them, but also keep your eyes open to unexpected opportunities, things you had never even considered. Trust me, they're always there.

This new mindset can help relax you. Whenever I find myself too focused on a particular path, it can create tension when obstacles arise. But if I instead keep my focus simply on the end result, I don't have to worry as much about *how* it will happen. I still take steps in the direction of my goal, but I'm open to the mysterious unknowns, as well.

I believe I'll get my desired results, but it might be in a way I never dreamed of.

I am open to new possibilities for making my dreams come true.

The unknown is exciting and fun. There's always something new!

I enjoy using my good energy to attract good things to me.

I'm jazzed to see what happens next.

Uncertainty injects more fun and color into my life.

Each day shows me amazing new surprises.

I wake up with wonder and awe about how my day will unfold.

TEA TIME #15

Are you taking enough time for yourself? Are you giving yourself enough space? Do you wake up in the morning and jump straight into your day, without enjoying a moment of peace first? Do you go to sleep at night rehashing the day in your mind, or obsessing on tomorrow's to-do list? It so, that's not magical living. You deserve better!

Now is the time to commit to making *you* a priority. And it starts with your self-talk.

Repeat the following affirmations, out loud if possible, while you drink your tea. Start making yourself a priority. When you make yourself a priority, your world changes, and everyone else's world around you improves, too.

So, I ask you... are you taking enough time for yourself?

I am worthy of taking time for me.

I love taking a pocket of time in the morning, and in the afternoon, just for myself.

I relish, and love, and cherish moments to myself.

I am happy when I have peace of mind, and this comes from taking time for myself.

I deserve time to rest my mind, body, and soul.

Deep breathing is a sign that I'm taking time. I breathe deeply now.

I am worthy of taking time for my precious self.

TEA TIME #16

Everyone is born with the potential for creativity. That means you, too.

Now, I'll be honest, I didn't spend the first 40 years of my life thinking this. Unfortunately. But that's ok, because I know it now. I went from thinking I didn't have a creative drop of blood in me, to feeling it sing in my bones.

And I know that *you* are creative, too. You just might have forgotten. But know this... you are creative. You were born with creativity. We all were. All children are creative. Some of us have just forgotten. But it's still in there, somewhere deep inside.

To unpack that creativity, there are things you can do. Creativity is simply connecting thoughts, ideas, and things to make something new. Or thinking of something you love and something you don't love, and imagining what it would mean if you put them together.

Give yourself material for your brain to work with, such as books, new experiences, skills, and encounters with a wide range of people. Fill your head with ideas of all shapes—including some ideas you *don't agree with*—and then let your mind do what it does naturally... which is creating something new, through comparing, connecting, and creating.

I am creative! Of course I am.

I was born with creativity, and it's inside me.

I love being creative.

Solving problems and putting things together is my specialty.

Invention and ingenuity come naturally to me.

My head is full of ideas of all shapes and sizes.

I'm a natural at being creative. We all are!

TEA TIME #17

People are always good company when they are doing what they really enjoy.

— SAMUEL BUTLER

Be excited that changing your self-talk will improve your personality. It will put you in a better mood. And when this happens, you'll find yourself showing up to places with a better energy, a higher vibe.

Which means people will enjoy being around you more. *Some will even say it to your face!* And not just people you've always known. Even some people you've just met will say, *"It's so nice being around you."*

Are you ready to give off a high vibe and make some new friends?

I love sharing my happy vibe with others.

Meeting new people puts a big grin on my face.

I walk into meetings eager to have a good time.

Loving myself and loving my life raises my vibration.

I am playful and happy, and others love being around me.

I'm living a heck of a good life, and it shows.

People love being around me, and I love being around people.

TEA TIME #18

The best way to use self-talk for rapid, lightning–fast change in your life is to combine your positive words and thoughts *with positive feelings in your heart.* Thinking and feeling make a powerful, magical combination.

Take a moment right now, and think about something you want that makes you feel happy.

Don't get bogged down in "how" the thing will manifest. (That engages a different part of your brain, a part that we're trying to sidestep for the time being.) You don't have to know the how. In time, it will be revealed.

Your job right now is simply thinking and feeling great. Feel super-duper amazing and good about having the things you want—imagine you have them now—and luxuriate in these good feelings, because you're worthy of them. That's it... just think great and feel great. That's the way to start living your magical life. Then, keep your eyes peeled. You'll soon start to see the blazing path to make your dreams come true.

I believe in my dreams to the fullest.

I think amazing words, and I feel amazing thoughts.

Feelings of love, awe, wonder, gratitude, and freedom drive my life.

I attract amazing things and people to me, because I think and feel great!

I am the master conductor of my life.

I'm in charge of my thoughts and feelings every waking moment.

I am happy. I am love. I am empowered. I am Me!

TEA TIME #19

You have an insanely awesome power inside of you, right now.

That power is *gratitude*. When you tap into gratitude, it changes you. It lifts your mood instantly. It elevates your energy. It even boosts your immune system. It's a legit way to get more sparkle into your life. Like, right now.

So, let's take massive advantage of this.

Take a moment, while you're drinking your tea, to think about anything and everything you're grateful for. Just start right now, saying the things out loud. Whisper your thanks to them. Take a sip of your tea, and say a few more. Take another sip, and say even more. It's fine to repeat things, if you like. Do this for five minutes... your five minutes of gratitude.

What are you grateful for?

I am grateful for manifesting my future.

I am grateful for my brain and my mind.

I am grateful for my tea.

I am grateful for the grass outside.

I am grateful for the cells in my body.

I am grateful for kindness in the world.

I am grateful for my life.

TEA TIME #20

Over the long term, the future is decided by optimists. To be an optimist, you don't have to ignore all the many problems we create; you just have to imagine improving our capacity to solve problems.

— KEVIN KELLY

People sometimes ask if I'm a bit too much of a Pollyanna. Um... no. (Lol.) And can I be honest? It's the biggest compliment to me.

Yes—I'm extremely optimistic, and it's my optimistic energy that helps me solve problems. (And honestly? It helps me get my head out of the sand on days I want it to bury it deeper.)

Overflowing with happiness doesn't mean ignoring issues, challenges, or problems. Rather, I take them head on, with a smile splittin' my mouth and a twinkling gleam in my eye. Like Kevin Kelly says in the quote above, I'm focused on "improving my capacity to solve problems," and I'm darn-tootin' proud of my optimistic mindset.

So don't ever let anybody tell you you're too optimistic. Tell them *you're just gettin' started!*

I'm an optimist, and this helps me solve problems. Heck yeah!

I love being cheerful despite circumstances. It keeps me upbeat! Woot!

Challenges have nothing on me and my bright attitude. Yeah, baby!

I am strong, vigilant, and I love being optimistic. Booyah!

I show up to my day with a big-ass smile plastered all over my face! Yessss!

I love my life! I love being happy! I love being an optimist! Watch me go!

I am an incredible person with a strong heart and high-vibe mind. Woohoo!

TEA TIME #21

I have a message from me to you:

Did you know that you were born to shine? You were born to stand tall. You were born to live your greatest life. You were born to be in charge of your life.

You were made for this. You were made for your dreams. They're yours, and they're yours for a reason.

Feel empowered, because you are in control of your destiny. It all starts with taking control of your mindset. You have that power and capability. It's all you, baby. Go for it.

So, that you know this important information, what are you going to do about it?

I am worthy of my desires. I was born to shine.

I love and approve of myself one million percent.

I am worthy of my own self-love, as I am RIGHT NOW.

I control my destiny. I have the power and the ability to go after
anything I desire.

I'm brilliant, and I love to learn. I'm a go-getter.

I am finesse! I am elegance! I am smart-n-sharp!

I'm living a completely new life powered by my amazing mindset.

TEA TIME #22

Have you ever considered the role discipline plays in your personal freedom? Strange, right? You might think the exact opposite, that discipline means a life of restriction. But discipline is how you acquire great habits, and these habits make you successful, give you choices, and ultimately freedom!

There are many ways to keep you flying along your incredible path. Sometimes it's inspiration, when you visualize magnificent results in your life. Sometimes it's motivation, because you're pumped up and rarin' to go. And sometimes it's discipline that keeps you marching on your path, day after day.

Because not every day is bedazzled with glitter. On challenging days, discipline keeps you moving. On those days you feel a bit lazy, your discipline says, *"No worries, scooch over, I'll drive."*

How do you get discipline? You commit to your actions. You commit to you. And you show up every day, for a while, no matter what. And this discipline of showing up makes habits. And these habits become automatic and effortless. And then, you no longer need discipline, and everything becomes easier.

I am disciplined. I am motivated. I am inspired.

Having discipline gives me freedom.

I can rely on myself, because I have discipline.

I love making good habits. They're time-savers.

My work is easier, because I'm disciplined.

I get magnificent results, and discipline helps me.

I show up, because my life is worthy. I am worthy.

TEA TIME #23

What's something really cool that's going on in your life right now?

Is there some new goal you're working on? A new book you're reading? Is it a new friend you've made? A vacation coming up?

During life's scruffy patches, remembering just one cool thing—any cool thing—can be enough to boost your energy and vibe. This can instantly steer your life in a new direction, simply by thinking about and appreciating one cool thing in your life.

Take a moment to think of one cool thing. Send waves of appreciation for this cool thing, and take a moment to smile.

Cool things happen for me all the time.

I'm a magnet for cool stuff. Bring it!

I play and dance through life, feeling cool and full of love.

I am so good at so many things.

I love. I share. I don't compare.

I have great things coming to me right now. I love having cool goals.

I am worthy of living, loving, and sharing.

TEA TIME #24

Visualizing is a key part to manifesting your most amazing life. In order to take steps toward the life you desire, and attracting it, you must have a picture of it in your mind.

If you were building a house, but you didn't have a blueprint, you'd never know where to start. It's the same with visualizing. In your mind, make a picture of what you want in your life. See it. Think about it. Love it. Believe it. Hold the picture in your mind, and let it captivate you. Get excited by the picture!

Let the pictures of your dreams wake up something wild in you.

I picture my most amazing life coming to me.

I'm whole, healed, and living a spectacular life.

Magic is all around me and inside me.

I see my life just the way I want it. I'm drawing it to me.

I slice through the mundane to find the marvelous.

My needs will always be met. I am capable. I am safe.

The world is open to me, and I see, think, feel, and believe in me!

TEA TIME #25

I've always loved change. As a kid, I bounced around between a couple different school districts, and I loved it every time. Perhaps it's because I'm a Gemini—lol. Regardless, change has always been fun to me.

But sometimes change comes in the form of *big* challenges, where you might feel scared, like the walls are closing in. Something changes in your life, and it makes you feel threatened.

In these times, *change means choice*. You have a choice for how you respond to the change. You have a choice to keep your mindset positive or negative. To see the change as scary and threatening, or as an opportunity for growth. *Because all change brings growth*. And you'll always get through any change. The choice is: Will you enjoy the ride while it happens, or will you be miserable? Are you going to keep your eyes open for opportunities and come up with a plan to power through, or are you going to freak out, bite your nails, and curl up into a ball and cry? *The choice is yours.*

What one person might see as crazy-scary, another person might see as an opportunity or an adventure. When change happens, you have a choice. How will you respond?

I love change. I embrace change.

Change means growth, which means opportunities.

Change comes with lessons I can use to help myself in the future.

I give change a giant bear hug.

I choose. I choose to see the rainbow, knowing it's there.

Ch-ch-ch-changes! I dance my way through changes.

I dig deep for gems, and I power through all change. I love it!

TEA TIME #26

When you want something in your life, you want to infuse your life with pictures of it, imagining the scene, like it's real and happening today—because this keeps you focused and keeps your energy driving toward it. And, honestly, it's fun, because you're thinking about the things you want, instead of focusing on the blah or stressing out.

The nifty little secret here is that, when you do this—*over and over and over*—it increases your belief in what you're picturing. It makes it feel more *real*. Which makes it *much* more likely to happen. Seeing your dreams clearly draws them to you faster.

To keep the pictures even more alive in your mind, look in magazines or online for pictures of the things you want. Surrounding yourself with these pictures keeps the image of your dream future at the forefront of your mind.

I believe in me, and I believe in my dreams. Oh yeah, baby!

I'm dreaming wide awake, and I'm in charge of what I make.

It's my life now. I'm on the rise. I'm starry-eyed.

My mind is where I come alive. I am triumphant!

I'm ready. I'm powerful. I'm incredible. I'm talented.

I'm a superstar. I'm rainbows, glitter, and shine.

Watch me go!

TEA TIME #27

With all this talk about doing positive self-talk as often as possible, it can feel stressful when you experience a moment of negative self-talk. Because you know it can be harmful, and in that moment, you might wonder if you're mucking up your efforts.

Well, let me ease your mind and say, it's all about *balance*. It's unrealistic to think you'll never have a negative thought or feeling. In fact, sometimes negative thoughts or feelings can trigger awareness of how amazing it is to have positive thoughts and feelings. It can be like shaking your shoulders to get you back on track.

All you need to do is keep the majority of your thoughts and feelings positive, and you'll continue to manifest that positivity in your life. Don't get hung up on a few hiccups once in a while. When you notice it happen, simply brush that dirt off your shoulders, get back up on your Pegasus, and fly-fly-fly!

I am calm. I have peace of mind.

I am kind and generous.

I am love, and I am gentle with myself.

I honor my mindset. It is so good to me.

I am strong, and all is well. Always.

I am overflowing with love and appreciation.

I look around and see all the brightness there is to see.

TEA TIME #28

We all have a one-track mind. Which means we can think about things that are beautiful, or we can think about things that are ugly. But we can't think about both the beautiful and ugly at the same time.

If you find yourself spiraling down a negative staircase in your head, then clap your hands, blink your eyes three times, and snap your fingers. Say, "Change!" (Scream it, chant it, sing it... whatever you want.)

In that moment, change your thoughts to something positive. It can be anything, from thoughts about your fur baby, or a TV show you want to see, or excitement about using self-talk to make your dreams come true. Or bacon. :)

And rest assured, as you think more positively, well, you'll think more positively! That's because you'll attract more to be positive about. You'll see more of the positive things around you that are always there.

What are your favorite positive things to think about? Make a list, and keep it handy, always ready to use.

I show the world what love looks like.

I show the world what awesome looks like.

I'm full of creativity and talent. They sing inside me.

I love my growth mindset. I'm unstoppable!

I easily come up with alternative ideas to any situation or problem.

I love inspiration, and inspiration loves me.

Life is pure magic, and so am I.

TEA TIME #29

You really do have the power to create your reality.

I have created the most wildly awesome life. All from my thoughts and words, which led to choices and actions. I believed so big and deep, because I loved my dreams so much. And they came true.

You have the power to create whatever it is that you commit to. You get to use your mind as a tool to design your best life. It is the most powerful tool in the world. You have everything you need within you right now, because it's *all in your mind*. And that's where you begin. You have the power to shape your perspective, in order to shape your life. By simply recognizing this, you take the first step. Begin your journey today.

My words mean more than ever before.

Today is a day for dreaming. Every day is!

I am power! Bam! Crackle! Shazam!

I'm full of fire, filled with inspiration and innovation.

I'm living a wildly awesome life. Thank you!

I love my dreams. Thank you!

I am confident and full of courage. Thank you!

TEA TIME #30

In difficult times, find something to be enthusiastic about, and you'll discover a nice, little source of joy.

Or come up with a goal. It can be any goal, such as to learn something new, or to get in better shape, or to improve some aspect of your life. To plan a future trip. To start reading a new epic fantasy series.

Anytime you feel stressed or challenged, find something to be enthusiastic about, and you will discover more joy amidst the circumstances.

I love being enthusiastic. Funnn!

Enthusiasm makes me sparkle and smile.

I'm here to play and rise above it all.

All is super well.

I am capable, and I'm doing it.

I love goals, plans, and promises to myself.

I paint my own world. I get to choose all the colors!

TEA TIME #31

Émile Coué was an incredible psychologist and pharmacist who introduced a popular method of self-improvement based on positive, repeated suggestion. He prescribed the mantra, *"Every day, in every way, I am getting better and better."*

So when I had COVID, this was my mantra, too, only I was saying, *"Every hour, in every way, I am getting better and better."*

It was amazing and totally helpful. It makes me giggle because, like, how simple. All through my fever, my aches, I kept thinking it. I kept whispering it. I kept believing it. (Well, I was doing that when I wasn't watching *Emily in Paris.* Haha.)

The result? My tango with COVID was over in a jiffy.

The mantra works for anything, not just health. How can you apply this line of positive thinking to your life? What do you want to get better and better at?

Every day, in every way, I am getting smarter and smarter.

Every hour, in every way, I am taking charge of my amazing brain.

Every second, in every way, I am loving myself more and more.

Every day, in every way, I am getting more and more creative.

Every day, in every way, my body heals and heals and heals.

Every day, in every way, I am getting richer and richer.

Every hour, in every way, I am calmer and calmer.

TEA TIME #32

If you want to be more appreciated in your life, make it your focus to appreciate. If you want more love in your life, make it your focus to love. If you want more gratitude in life, make it your focus to be grateful.

Whatever it is you want in life, make that thing first and foremost in your mind. It's that simple. Everything you want always starts with you.

What do you want more of in your life?

What are you going to do to get more of it?

I am here to prosper, and I see prosperity all around me.

I am here to love, and I shoot arrows of love at everything.

I am here to live my legendary life, and I see magic every day.

I am here. Everything I want starts with me.

When I focus on happiness, I see more happiness. Happy!

When I look for smiles, I smile more. Smiles!

All is supremely well!

TEA TIME #33

A fast track to feeling AMAZING is altruism... helping someone else, simple acts of kindness or giving. Compassion. Help. Love. Altruism is a longevity vitamin, because the people who do for others, in any regard, find themselves happier and healthier.

In fact, science shows that *giving* plays an active role in reward and pleasure. No wonder it feels so awesome to be altruistic. It's a first-class ticket to magical living.

Take a moment, right now, and think of just one person that you can help. It might be a co-worker, or a family member. Maybe a neighbor. It could be sending them a text message telling them how much you appreciate them. You could bake them cookies, or buy them a cup of coffee, or simply give them a few bucks and say, your next coffee is on me!

It could be giving them a hug and a smile. Or a compliment. When we lighten the burdens of others and uplift another's spirit, we take our own energy to beautiful, new levels that pulse love through the world.

Being kind to others is my way of life. I love being kind.

I have a generous heart, and this feels so wonderful.

Sharing with others makes me smile. Yesss! Sharing is caring!

I improve my world and my life when I'm kind and giving.

Helping. Love. Compassion. Altruism. These make my life magical.

The world appreciates when I lend a helping hand. This is the way to live.

It's a great day for helping others. It's a great day to be generous. Right now!

TEA TIME #34

Expectation is a great mind trick. If you expect something magnificent to happen, you're much more likely to perceive it happening! Which means you'll be more relaxed. Your hands will be open, and you won't grasp so tightly. Expecting something improves your belief in it, because in your mind, it's a done deal.

So expect great things, and expect to enjoy your life.

Because you will.

I expect the best, because I'm worthy of the best.

I live a first-class life of fun, joy, and love. I am here to play HUGE!

My thought process is perfect.

My sparkling energy and fiery intuition guide me.

It is safe to follow my truth. I am safe.

I manifest everything I want.

I live in a state of marvel, awe, and expectation of the best. Always.

TEA TIME #35

Your emotions are your fortune teller. Your emotions are the canaries in the coal mine. Your emotions are your compass and your direction.

As you know, your emotions have a wide range, and having as many positive emotions as possible is a great recipe to happier living. But if your emotion is low or negative, it's like that canary is chirping, *"Chirp-chirp! Pay attention!"*

Anytime you want to know where your day is headed (or your life!), simply look into your heart, and see what emotions are stirring through you.

How are you feeling *right now*?

My life is interesting, and I am interesting!

I am here to tap into my own beautiful, shining soul. Tap-Tap-Tap!

I listen to my own happy truth.

I create what I am called to create. It's my power.

I know in my soul what works best for me, and I follow it. I listen.

Attracting my great life is easy, and I start with my energy.

Bliss sparkles all around me, all over me, and all through me.

TEA TIME #36

When you feel yourself drowning in uncertainty and doubt, then you need to do one thing: Turn your focus to what could go "right" about the situation. Just do it.

Think to yourself: What's possible? What could be good here? What could this turn into that I'm not considering?

Run through as many scenarios as it takes for you to start to feel more calm. Sometimes this exercise yields a big smile. Other times, it simply relaxes you, because you realize the situation wasn't even as bad as you thought.

I turn my focus to all of the incredible possibilities, and all the good I will discover.

I stretch my mind and my eyes to discover something new.

Whatever I am destined to do will be a success.

I go from success, to success, to success. It's how I roll.

I focus on what lights me up. I shine. I'm riding a shimmering rainbow!

The road is paved in gold, and I light my path.

I'm thankful for my perseverance and awesomeness. Woohoo!

TEA TIME #37

So much of good health and wellness comes straight from your brain.

Take gratitude, for instance... did you know that gratitude boosts your immune system? Or belief... believing in your body's ability to heal itself is *powerful*. There's a whole field of science that studies the placebo effect, when believing that a "dummy" pill will work, and then it actually works! What's going on there? How amazing that, just because your brain thinks it's real medicine, it can cause your body to respond as if it truly is real. *Whaaat?* Mind blown.

Take full advantage of your subconscious anytime you get sick, or have a headache, or PMS cramps. Use your mindset for gratitude and for *belief in your body to heal,* and then go find things in life to enjoy and to support your body being relaxed, which further supports your incredible healing.

I am worthy of health and wholeness.

My body is a powerful, self-healing machine.

I am full of good vibes that prime me for healing.

I feel whole. I am healing. I feel amazing.

I glow, from my head to my toes.

Heal, body, heal. I love you so much, wonderful body.

My body has smiling emoji zipping all through me, healing.

TEA TIME #38

Inner guidance always provides peace.

It's when you're forcing something that things get harder. When you push hard, circumstances push back hard. Instead, step back and ask yourself, *What do I really think about this?* And you let all restrictive opinions fall away. Stop "trying." Walk away from your list of pros and cons... there is no scoresheet. There is no need to over-analyze.

Instead, you loosen up. Relax your shoulders. You take a deep breath. Engulf yourself in silence. Reach inside, and feel your intuition speak. Listen to what it's telling you.

Your inner guidance always tries to communicate with you. But if you don't have silence, you won't hear it. If you're constantly bombarded by social media, or articles, or news —you won't hear your own, powerful inner voice. But when you stop overwhelming your mind with opinions and outside noise, you can hear your inner guidance speaking to you.

The answer always comes when your mind is clear.

I have peace of mind. Silence is my ally.

My intuition guides me, and I love the ride.

It is easy for me to be quiet and let my intuition speak.

I honor my breath and the quiet that brings me answers.

I am curious, and my intuition answers. I love being curious.

I am a calm and at peace. I breathe in the unknown and come alive.

A breakthrough idea is coming to me now. I'm quiet. I'm happy. I'm ready.

TEA TIME #39

When you have a positive mindset, you see things more clearly. When you have an upbeat attitude, it's easier to make decisions. Why does this happen? Because your optimism creates an air of detachment, a feeling of knowing that things have a way of working out, and a vibe that knows opportunities are always around.

It's a closed, negative mindset that closes doors.

Keeping your mind open will always make life easier.

I love having an open mind.

Doors of opportunity are all around me.

I love to experiment and play, and curiosity makes me smile.

I am worthy. We are all worthy.

I'm an alchemist cracking open my own power. I am energy!

Abundance is everywhere I turn. It's here. It's there. It's everywhere!

I wrap myself in worthiness, and worthiness hugs me back.

TEA TIME #40

Here are two things master manifesters *never* do:

- They don't let doubt drive them.
- They don't let negative emotions rule their day.

Here are two things master manifesters *always* do:

- They drive their life fueled by belief in themselves.
- They let positive emotions rule their day.

Which are you?

I am a master manifester, because I believe in myself.

I am a master manifester, because my energy radiates positivity!

I am a master manifester, because I know the way.

I am a master manifester, because I'm worthy.

I am a master manifester, because I am patient.

I am a master manifester, because I am full of love.

I am a master manifester, because I dance with my life.

TEA TIME #41

I have a safe room inside my mind. It has hot pink walls and a sassy, leopard-print couch.

Whenever the world tosses me a curveball... or when I'm dumbfounded on how to proceed with something... or when I'm scared... I close my eyes, and I go lounge in there, in that room in my mind, all safe and relaxed.

You see, it's chill here. Peaceful. No preconceived ideas of what's right or wrong. No requirements. No deadlines.

And once I'm feeling like myself again, I stretch, roll my shoulders, and I get back to being a badass. Living my magical life.

What does the safe room in your mind look like?

I find my own peace, anytime I want.

I am confident, and safe, and solid as a rock.

Out of the shadows and into the bright light... here I come.

I light my own fuse. I strike my own match, because I am a badass!

I trust myself to find my way.

I trust my magical mind to get back on my path.

I am magnificent.

TEA TIME #42

Sometimes it takes making a big change to shake things up and radically alter your behavior.

Perhaps it means moving to a new house. Or getting rid of your old furniture. (And not replacing it!) Or decluttering your wardrobe. Sometimes it means drastically ripping something out of your life, tearing it off all at once, like a Band-Aid. Sometimes it means jumping into something big with both feet and changing your whole life.

Sometimes, this big shake-up in your life creates a huge wave that is actually *easier* to surf, because it's so massive, so epic, that it overwhelms everything else, wiping out all of life's little distractions.

Is there some big change you need to make in your life?

I love change! And when I go big, I go super big!

I am building my dreams by showing up every day.

I am brave. I am full of the juiciest juice! I sparkle.

I can do it. I am doing it! Yeeeeehaw!

I am dazzled by my own capabilities and competence.

I wow myself every day with my resilience.

I am called to live my epic, magical life.

TEA TIME #43

When you ask the universe for signs, don't ignore them when they show up.

— HEIDI DELLAIRE

I've been using my positive self-talk to manifest more and more prosperity over the years.

And there came a time when an opportunity arrived. But I wasn't totally feeling it. So I passed on it. Well, the opportunity came back a second time, only stronger. *Buuuut*, I still wasn't feeling it. So I passed on it again. Naturally, I wondered, *Am I doing the right thing?* I didn't have a crystal ball telling me what to do.

Well. Funny thing. The opportunity came back. Again. And this time, it was a *much bigger* opportunity than the previous two *combined*. At which point, I looked up at the stars and said, *"Are you trying to tell me something?"*

So I jumped. I took the offer. And I didn't look back.

Is there something you're hitting the snooze button on? Is there something that keeps tapping on your soul to do?

I trust myself to receive.

I am prosperous and confident.

I pay attention to the signs that are here to guide me.

I listen to my intuition.

I know that, whatever I choose, I'm always a rockstar, and I make my own way in life.

I pay attention to my feelings. I mind my energy.

I am grateful. I am grateful. I am grateful.

TEA TIME #44

Gratitude adds *golden pixie dust to my life.*

It makes me happier. It boosts my mood on any day, dark or light. And it will for you, too. It makes life magical.

Use gratitude as a tool in your happiness toolbox. Give your life gratitude now, and this will make manifesting the stuff you want so much easier.

The more gratitude you feel, the bigger you smile, and the faster you can make your dreams come true—all of them. Gratitude pours jet fuel into the gas tank of your magical life.

What do you want more of? What are you grateful about?

I am grateful for the money in my bank account, today.

I am grateful for the love I have inside me, now.

I am grateful for the energy I have.

I am grateful for the relationships I have.

I am grateful for my comfy pillow, my home, my tea, and for me.

I am grateful for my amazing self-talk!

I am grateful for waking up to another glorious day.

TEA TIME #45

Wouldn't it be amazing to live a life with ZERO stress? But the truth is, stress makes us resilient. A little bit of stress is actually a good thing.

Think about it... when you go to the gym and lift weights, what are you really doing? You're stressing your body. And then you take the next day off to let those muscles recover. And this recovery is how your body gets stronger. In fact, getting stronger *requires* the rest. It's absolutely necessary.

The same thing happens with mental stress: It's good to have a little. It helps us grow stronger. It's not the stress that's bad, it's how you handle the stress, and *how you recover* from it. This stress-recovery cycle is what makes you resilient. And you do that by getting quality recovery time. This is completely different than the dangerous *chronic* stress, which never ends, and recovery never happens.

The next time you're stressed, take a breath. If you've had a freak out, that's ok. The important thing is getting through it (use your self-talk to help!), and then take time for recovery. Create a ritual or a reward. Take an hour for yourself. Exercise or walk. Find a way to help you recover after stress happens, and over time, you'll build up an insane amount of resilience.

I grow from stressful situations. I am always getting better at life.

I take time to recover, because it makes me stronger.

I am worthy of recovery time. I love recovering. It feels phenomenal.

If I fall down, I take a deep breath, take some time to recover, and I get back up.

My stress and recovery cycle is magic, and so am I.

When shit happens, I chuckle and handle it with grace and power.

Hear me ROAAAR!

TEA TIME #46

What are your dreams?

Make a list and put it where you can see it. Perhaps write them on your phone, or on a giant poster board, so they're in your face morning and night. And write one dream each per sticky note, and put them all over your house. Talk about them several times a day to yourself, or your partner, or a friend. Or even to your pet. I talk about my dreams to my dog all the time. It's especially great when he cocks his head and listens. Sometimes he even wags his tail... pretty sure he's giving me his support! :)

When you keep yourself hyped up about your dreams, you increase your belief that they'll happen. You keep the momentum going! So every day, dedicate time to dream about your dreams. Imagine them with full detail, attention, and intention. Flow your energy and vibes straight to them.

What are your dreams? Say them out loud, right now, so you can be crystal clear.

I infuse my dreams with my fullest energy.

I think about my dreams all day long.

I pay attention to my dreams, because they're worthy.

I am living a blessed life. This is a blessed day!

I have time for everything I want to do today.

My dreams are coming to me. I can feel it. I love it!

I am the master of my magical dreams.

TEA TIME #47

Sometimes life is sailing along, and... *thwack!*... something happens. You're jarred. You're shaken.

Well, that can happen. The world has curveballs and wrecking balls.

So here's what I do when something shitty happens.

I think, *"F*************ck!"*

(Sometimes I scream this, or I sing it in my most operatic opera voice.)

And then I say, *"Ok, now let me find my happy."*

The point is, let the energy of the moment flow through you, and release it. And then it's gone, and you can get back up and keep on going.

I find my happy, because that's how I roll!

Only good lies before me.

I am in the right place, at the right time, doing the right thing.

Everything is perfect. I feel fabulous.

I am grateful for my health.

I love my life, and life loves me.

I am worthy of everything I want. I am amaze-balls!

TEA TIME # 48

There's very little that's more important than feeling great. Most days, this is my natural flow.

But on the days when I don't have that amazing buzz? I ask myself, simply, *"What will it take to make me feel great?"* And the answer is the same every time: I start with my words. I start out by saying *"I feel amazing."* Even if I don't! But *shhh!* Don't tell my mind that because it doesn't know. *Wink wink.*

Next, I picture my dreams, and I visualize what I want in my life. What goal am I working toward? The picture feels good to imagine. And I'm intimately aware of the power my mind has to make my dreams come true. *I feel it in my bones.*

And I remind myself about all the things I've already accomplished using the power of my mind. It makes it easy to hitch a ride on that magical train. Of course, it took practice to get here, but this process works.

Each new day, I receive wonderful new surprises.

I am very, very special. And I deserve a wonderful life.

My good comes from everywhere, everything, and everyone!
Thank you!

I like me. I like who I am. I feel good about myself.

I'm on the right track. The magic track. The happy track.

Abundance, love, and prosperity in all forms are drawn to me!

There is no one else in the world like me. :)

TEA TIME #49

Remember gentleness. Take time to be gentle in your day. Gentle with your magic. Gentle with your power. Gentle with life. Think flowers, butterflies, and all things dainty and sweet.

Look at yourself in the mirror, and whisper words of gentle strength. Words of love. Words that uplift, like a soft breeze under your wings.

Some days we plow ahead, we charge, we ride that big wave with gusto and verve. And other days, we float, we soar, and we glide effortlessly.

Both are magic.

Both are useful.

Having both keeps us balanced.

I am sweetness and lace, pearls, and beauty.

I'm seeing my life with fresh eyes, like a newborn fawn in the forest.

I revel in the raw, the unprocessed, the new. I'm here. I'm ready.

I have a cool perspective on the world, I love viewing it from different angles.

I'm friendly, kind, and gentle with myself.

I'm friendly, kind, and sweet with others.

I am perfect just the way I am.

TEA TIME #50

Take your focus off you for a day. Put your focus on others.

For every person you encounter, make your objective the following: *I want this person to leave our interaction feeling better than when we began.*

What a fun day when you do this!

When you make this your goal—for other people to feel joy, just by being with you—you'll beam a whole new rainbow shine. And so will they.

Here are a few tips:

- Tell some jokes, and make them laugh.
- Listen actively and encourage them.
- Compliment them. Make them feel noticed.
- Give them a huge hug, and hold it longer than usual.
- Ask them how you can help them.
- Tell them how much you appreciate them.
- If someone is serving you, give them an epic tip, and write a nice note on the slip!

I love helping others.

Helping others helps me.

Giving feels so good.

I love to love.

I am generous. I am generous. I am generous.

I am an excellent listener, and people love this about me.

I give great eye contact and my full attention to people.

TEA TIME #51

When I entered the hospital, I was prepared for one leg to be amputated.... But since I have been in the hospital, I have discovered that I must have both legs removed. ... I have been here in my bed thinking about all the wonderful things I'm going to do with my hands when I go home from the hospital.

— STEPHEN POST AND JILL NEIMARK, *WHY GOOD THINGS HAPPEN TO GOOD PEOPLE*

Wow. 'Nuff said, right?

I look on the bright side of everything.

I see the rainbows in any storm.

If there is darkness, I glow. I glow for me. I glow for others.

It's a great day for dreaming. Every day is.

Good things happen to me, because I feel good.

I adore my positive eyes, I love my curious mindset, and I focus on the good. This makes a great life.

TEA TIME #52

Laughter is legit magic. I probably don't need to tell you that, because when you laugh, you feel epic! A good belly laugh is an injection of immune boosting, star-shining goodness. An extended laughing session compares to exercise—your abs and face even get sore! Laughter makes you feel magical, because you secrete all kinds of delicious, mood-enhancing endorphins and neurochemicals.

Make laughter *a core value*, and you'll consciously seek more things to laugh about. Make it your default to chuckle at mistakes, even when it feels unnatural. Start *ha-ha-ha-ing* anyway, and watch what it does to you. I know, crazy, but just pretend. Seriously, trust me... pretend things are funny. Your mind hardly knows the difference when you do that.

After doing this for a while, you start to lighten up whenever something less than ideal happens! It feels like magic, but you've really just trained your brain to respond to things in a new way.

Laughter is a kiss on my lips.

I'm dragons, fairies, twinkles, and stars.

I love laughing! Tee hee hee! Ha ha ha!

I'm on a magic carpet ride, swooshing through the starry sky.

I'm laughing and playing, feeling so lovely and high.

I laugh every day. Laughing is funny, and I have a great sense of humor.

I am grateful for laughter, and I'm worthy of laughing!

TEA TIME #53

Did you know the chimichanga was invented in Tucson, Arizona, when somebody accidentally dropped a burrito into the deep fryer?

A mistake.

A whoops-a-daisy.

And a food that came to be a favorite for millions of bellies.

There are so many stories like this, of products and creativity coming from mistakes and mishaps. That's the magic of mistakes.

I learn great things when I make mistakes.

I can make big money from the mistakes I make.

Mistakes and mishaps provide some of life's biggest flashes of insight.

I blow kisses to my mistakes.

A big whoops can become a big discovery!

I appreciate my mistakes. They make me smarter and stronger.

I am brave, and I love trying new things, even if I mess it up!

TEA TIME #54

Have you ever considered that your life, your relationships, your success, and your abundance are supposed to be massively greater than you've allowed yourself to imagine?

Most people have a limited idea of how great their life could be. They do this by limiting their thoughts. Thinking small. So I'm here to shake your shoulders and get in your face. *Think big, baby!*

Don't settle. Don't underestimate yourself or the power of your mind. Open it, like a parachute. Big. Wide-open. Epic. Expansive. Can you see it all? How big are you willing to go with your dreams?

How about ten times bigger? So, if you thought "a million dollars," how about going for ten million? If you thought "a nice romance where my partner has good manners and nice hair," how about someone who massages your shoulders while you go to sleep, surprises you with love notes, and supports your every desire? You thought "open a boutique," how about starting retail dynasty?

When you dream big, you naturally start to *think* big. And this changes what you focus on, and helps you discover ways to make the big dreams come true—which you wouldn't have thought of otherwise, had you not started thinking big.

I love thinking big. My life is big.

I am a big thinker. An epic dreamer. An unstoppable doer.

I am worthy of my biggest, most incredible dreams.

My huge dreams yield huge inspirations.

I am unlimited! I am an explorer!

I am ready for it all.

I do anything I put my heart and mind to. It's an amazing feeling!

TEA TIME #55

Regardless of your past. Regardless of your history. You can start living a better life today.

Right now.

How do I know this? Because I did it myself! My past was drowned in struggles. My past was full of cloudy, dark days. My past had a young woman who didn't know her worth.

But your past doesn't matter. Because you get to create a new you, starting today. With words. The words and thoughts you say about your life. Your self-talk is the key to your success. It's the key to your very own magical kingdom.

Change the story of your life with new words. Right now...

I'm in the right place, at the right time, doing the right thing.

I create my me, today. I choose the words to transform myself.

I'm tenacious. I'm smart. I'm kind.

I focus on choices that give me peace.

I focus on words that make me strong.

I'm living a completely new life of my own creative design.

I am full of optimism, and I'm passionate about my destiny.

TEA TIME #56

Overflow... I just *love* that word.

I love the images it conjures in my mind. Use this word to imagine a gushing overflow of anything you desire... overflow of love... overflow of self-worth... overflow of money... overflow of health... overflow of gratitude...

What overflow are you thinking about now?

I am worthy of an overflow of love.

An overflow of money feeeels so good.

I am overflowing with ideas and creativity.

I gush and overflow with self-love.

My confidence is overflowing. I am courageous. I am brave.

Waterfalls of sparkles overflow through me right now, as I read this.

I feel an overflow of health lighting up my body with radiant energy.

TEA TIME #57

I maintain a mind full of awe, and an expectation of excitement—which keeps the magic coming my way, every day.

When I go to sleep at night, I say out loud, *"I wonder what exciting things will happen tomorrow."*

When my eyes pop open the next morning, and I'm rubbing the sleep out of them, I say out loud, *"I wonder what awesome things will happen today!"*

YOWZA! This mindset really works. It's playful. It's expectant. And it instantly curls my lips into a sparkly grin. And it can deliver amazing, exciting things to you day after day.

I am full of wonder and awe, all day long.

I love asking: What exciting things will happen today?

I fall asleep every night with feelings of peace and wonder.

I wake up in the morning with smiles and curiosity.

I have generosity and joy zipping through my mind.

I am grateful for this attitude, which makes my life more magical.

I am full of wonder and awe... all day long. Yessss!

TEA TIME #58

How to go from thinking to manifesting: Think something, and take action *by pretending it's true.* For example, I think, *I'm a bestselling author,* and I picture it in my mind. Then, I go next level. Okay, so I feel a little silly sharing this with you, but being vulnerable is an act of self-love, so here it goes...

I *pretend*, just like a kid. I have moments of *total make-believe,* where I role-play at my desk. Like, I imagine an email coming in, congratulating me on making *The New York Times* best sellers list. I even had my husband create a Photoshop mockup of the list with one of my books on it! I see it every day, and it *feeeels* real!

This kind of thing, this total make-believe, is so much fun. And fun is high-vibe. And high-vibing is *manifesting juice,* because it deepens your belief in yourself and what's possible.

What do you want in your life? How will you play make-believe today, to imagine it's already true?

I make-believe my way to my dreams.

I am a shimmer-shimmer me, confident and sparkling.

I radiate good times and play my way to my goals.

I have fun. I'm a sparkling-bright child of the universe.

I have playdates with myself. We imagine BIG things.

My color shines and lights my way.

I have seriously powerful manifesting juice swirling through my veins.

TEA TIME #59

What is the most prominent picture in your mind today? And what does it feel like when you picture it? What is the picture's *energy*? Because, guess what? Whatever you're seeing and feeling, that's the direction of your tomorrow.

You must always remember that your most prominent thoughts determine the direction of your life. They determine what good or bad you see. But here's the awesome news! You can make sure it's something good *right now*.

Simply think of a picture in your mind of what you want in your life—happiness, health, calm, wealth, being loved—and picture yourself in one of them, and keep this picture as your most prominent mental image, as often as you can, for as many days as you can.

Want a bigger life? Make a bigger picture.

Be definite. Be specific.

Persist in feeling joy, cheer, and optimism.

Expect it.

I hang pictures in my mind of my dream life. I think about them all the time. I see them when I close my eyes.

My thoughts determine my life. It's that simple.

If I want a bigger life, I make a bigger picture. There is no limit!

I persist in joy and optimism. This makes my every day magical.

My morning is full of cheer. My afternoon is full of joy. My evening is full of peace.

I am living the most amazing life in the most amazing way.

When I want something, I think it, speak it, feel it, and believe it.

TEA TIME #60

Magical Living Tip:

If you regard yourself as "needing" things to happen, then that's the energy you bring to your life. Instead, start with elevated emotions like happiness, love, and gratitude, and those will help you make your dreams come true—without ever having a desperate, *needy* feeling.

Why? Because a needy mind courts lack and scarcity. It borders on whiny. Definitely not magical. Much better to believe that the things you "want" are coming at you, at the speed of a freight train.

When I was buried in debt, I never let myself fall prey to the line of thinking "I need money!" Instead, I chose excitement about all the money I knew would come to me. I had no idea how I would get out of debt... but I believed I would. And that belief *brought me peace.*

And today? I'm happy with the debt gone, of course. But the money didn't bring me happiness. My happiness helped bring me the money.

I believe in the power of belief.

I show up to my life, waking up to the magic that's all around me.

I choose happiness, no matter the circumstances.

I feel loved, and I love—deeply and daily.

When I have love, I have wings. I sparkle, I shine, I fly.

I'm a gem. I'm unique. I'm kindness. I'm awe.

My mindset is the key to my freedom. My peace of mind.

TEA TIME #61

When I look back on my past, I see the crazy-difficult challenges and struggles I had. But I don't have those struggles anymore, because my brain is different.

Strange as it may seem, I look back fondly at those times. They gave me grit and determination that I get to use today. I didn't know it at the time, but mistakes and tough lessons give you experience, and experience makes you better at life.

If you're struggling with something, take advantage of the struggle by digging deeper and finding your grit. You *will* come out of your current situation. That's a given. But whether you come out shining or gloomy is largely determined by your attitude.

Once you realize that challenges make you strong, then new challenges don't faze you as much. You waltz through them with a sense of calm and grace. Sometimes you even laugh at them. And this is a beautiful way to live.

I want change, so here I am, ready to go.

My goals are manifesting before my eyes. I create my reality.

I am the master conductor of my life. Watch me go!

I vibrate in a beautiful energy so high, that greatness pours straight into my life.

Something wild is awakening in me, right now.

Joy is my default. Happiness is my normal state of mind.

TEA TIME #62

"Watch your mouth!"

As a kid, I didn't like it when my mom said this to me, when I spoke poorly about something or someone. But I sure do appreciate it now.

And I say it to you: *Watch your mouth!*

Which is another way of saying *Watch your words. Notice your thoughts.* Always pay attention. Don't get lazy with your emotions. Be strong and vigilant. Choose words that benefit your life. Choose words that uplift you and motivate you. Choose words that make you feel good!

Choose words that deliver you to the life of your dreams.

Watch your mouth! :)

I am worthy of all the love in the world.

I am patient, and I understand that love is always the answer.

I am living my legendary life. It is my birthright.

I hold the key to the achievement of anything I want.

YEEEEEEEAAAAAAHHHHHHH!

I love sharing with others. I love being generous.

We are all connected. Thank you, world.

TEA TIME #63

Did you know that you can *start over* anytime you want?

With your whole life, or with one little part. Why not take as many re-dos as you want? It's ok to have made mistakes. It's perfectly fine to do a 180 from where you are now.

You only need to make the decision.

Is there anything in life you just want to do over? To try again with a fresh mindset? Maybe try a new diet? A new hobby? A new style? A new relationship? A new career?

It's liberating to think that you can grant yourself permission to start over, to give yourself a fresh start, at anything, anytime.

I build my kingdom from scratch. Anytime I want.

I drink from the wild air.

I rise every time.

I am alert. I am ready. I am here.

I am always in the right place at the right time.

I love my days.

I was born for this. I hit the gas 'n go.

TEA TIME #64

Here's a fun list of ways to keep your beautiful relationships growing, fun, and energized. Appropriate for romantic partners, friends, and family.

1. Do fun stuff together!
2. Watch funny movies together!
3. Hug! A lot!
4. Communicate regularly, like *obsessively*!
5. Go someplace new together.
6. Learn something new together.
7. Compliment each other daily, and pump each other up!

I love my relationships, and I appreciate them.

I love doing new things with my friends.

Hugging my family feeeels so great.

I give out compliments freely and generously.

I trust my relationships. I am safe in my relationships.

I am loyal, and I honor my word.

My relationships are worthy of fun, and love, and time!

TEA TIME #65

When I let go of who I was, I was able to become who I wanted to be.

— Taoist proverb

I first heard this years ago, and man, did it ever hit my core. I was in a dark time in my life. I wanted to change, to be someone else, because what I'd been doing up until then wasn't working. I wasn't sparkling.

But at the time, all I knew was the old me. And I had to work up the courage to give her up, in order to become the reborn butterfly that I am today.

I admit, it wasn't easy. I even had a breakdown. But I got through it with perseverance and belief, and I had my breakthrough. I'd believed something better was on the other side, but I had to cross over that mountain of change to get there. I had to let go of the old me. But I kept going, thank goodness, because I'm happier than ever now.

I let go, in order to become.

I let go, in order to become.

I release, in order to transform.

I release, in order to transform.

I am building a new me.

I am doing what it takes.

I keep on going.

TEA TIME #66

Transforming into a new person takes time.

Perhaps you want to have more confidence, or be more generous, or have stronger will... these all take time. It takes time and repetition, reprogramming your subconscious to turn you into the new you that you want to become.

It will happen. But it takes commitment. It takes showing up on a regular basis and telling your subconscious exactly what you want. It's always listening and waiting for your instructions. Your beautiful subconscious mind will respond powerfully to the directions you give it. But it will take time and patience.

It's like planting seeds to grow some basil in your kitchen; the basil doesn't burst into a plant overnight. But with watering, and sunlight, and love, it will grow, and you will manifest your delicious basil.

Give yourself the proper direction, frequently and consistently.

Give yourself time.

You *will* transform. I promise.

I see my incredible potential, and I tap into this every day. I am living an incredible life.

I achieve more and more each day, because I know I can. I see the good in me, the sparkling and the brave.

I am committed to living my best life.

My subconscious mind is where my power resides, and I feed it the right fuel by saying and thinking the right words.

I am generous with myself and my time. I have an abundance of time, patience, and love.

I deserve to live a phenomenal life, and I think my way toward it every day, step by step!

I am calm. I am love. I am excitement. I am ready!

TEA TIME #67

You can't start a fire without a spark.

— BRUCE SPRINGSTEEN

I was watching American Idol one night, and the featured artist was Bruce Springsteen. One of the contestants sang the song *Dancing in the Dark*, which contains the lyric quoted above, and I immediately thought about affirmations, self-talk, and transformation.

It's the perfect metaphor, about what a simple affirmation can do. An affirmation is the spark that starts the fire.

When you want to make a change, to get that ball rolling, *start with a spark.*

And then, watch the flame grow and gain momentum. Start your passionate happy fire, with a sweet, little spark.

I am kindness and love. This sparks my transformation.

I am full of passion and fire for my dreams.

I am generous. Spark!

I see the good. Spark! Spark!

I choose to be free. Spark! Spark! Spark!

I choose to see the happy, and this ignites my own happiness.

I am grateful for starting my fire from one little spark. Yes!

TEA TIME #68

When you find yourself in a situation, do you find yourself looking at everything that's right there in front of you? You know, the obvious? Sometimes, answers *are* obvious. But when they're not, having a narrow focus can limit your options. You fail to see the *non-obvious.*

Or do you consider alternatives? The crazy-sounding *what-ifs*? Do you brainstorm possibilities, getting creative about what could be?

I love talking about all the different things that *could be,* or that something could turn into, or other changes for the better. Even for something that's already good, and I like imagining ways it could be even better.

So when you're faced with a tough challenge, and the solution isn't presenting itself, take it to the next level, injecting crazy wonder into the situation. Big living comes from big thinking... so don't just see things the way they are.

See them as they *could be*!

I am a treasure hunter, looking for buried treasure in the least likely places!

I explore under rocks and look for possibilities.

I ask questions and imagine using the question, What is possible?

I enjoy thinking outside the box. It helps me manifest my magical life.

I'm a pro at thinking big, because I practice big thinking every day.

I am amazing. I am love. We are all amazing. We are all love!

Wild wonder and a sense of awe move my feet and drive me forward. I am having so much fun!

TEA TIME #69

I enjoy money.

It's not the money itself, it's what it means. For some, it means security. For others, prestige. For me, money means freedom, and I'm *all about* freedom. Money means having choices. More opportunities. The ability to help others.

Does money mean happiness? No, not directly. I live my life according to a rule I call *unconditional happiness*, which means I find my happiness no matter what's going on, including how much money I have. But let's be clear: Money sure does add some sweet-n-sass. And some comforts.

I share this with you because, when something is important to you, then it's worth thinking about *why* it's important. Knowing why you want something is essential to manifesting it. Whether that's love, or health, or travel, or a new skill, or a whole new career. For today's script, it's about money. Feel free to modify this for anything you're currently working toward.

I have a great relationship with money.

I appreciate money.

I deserve money, because I am deserving.

I am worthy of abundance. We all are.

I love money and all the wonderful things I can do with it.

Thank you, prosperity!

Thank you, money!

TEA TIME #70

Deliverance.

Gosh, another great word that I love.

Deliverance means being set free or being rescued. When you think about your self-talk, I want you to connect it with the idea of *deliverance*. Because, through changing your mindset to one of love, awe, and gratitude, you will literally set yourself free.

You will *rescue yourself*.

It's the most incredible feeling, the empowerment that comes from this. *Woo-whee!* I get all breathy and teary-eyed just writing about it.

When you take charge of your perspective, your mind, your words, your thoughts, your reactions to things... you get deliverance.

I rescue myself with my words and my thoughts.

Deliverance rushes through me.

Freedom is my song.

I have the most incredible feeling inside me.

It's my time. My empowerment is here.

I am confident. I am calm. I am taking the right steps.

I can do anything. I am free.

TEA TIME #71

Waku waku (わくわく, pronounced *whauk whauk*) is a great Japanese term. I just love how it sounds! (I mean, how could you not?) But I especially love its meaning: thrilling, excitement, or to be thrilled or excited. In this way, waku waku is tightly linked with positive self-talk.

In my book, *Coffee Self-Talk*, I teach how to write your own self-talk, and occasionally adding an unfamiliar or unusual term into your script injects a bit of fun into your affirmation.

It makes your brain sit up and take notice, and it creates a stronger picture, or association. So, when you write your positive self-talk, consider taking a term like "happy" or "success" and looking up how to say them in a foreign language. You might discover something that lights you up! *Shazam!*

I'm thrumming with waku waku joy.

I am full of waku waku about my projects.

Waku waku for all the magic of life.

I love my waku waku days.

I am waku waku.

I am worthy of waku waku!

All is wonderfully waku waku well!

TEA TIME #72

Nola is a celebrity of sorts in the world of successful aging. She will tell you she was born in 1911, but she says, 'I don't keep track of my age.' Widespread recognition came when she earned her college degree at age ninety-five. That was, in fact, a world record, but she went even further, earning her master's degree at age ninety-eight.

— ROGER LANDRY, *LIVE LONG, DIE SHORT*

Let this sink in and inspire you.

I love learning. I will keep learning all my life.

Age is just a number. It's how I act that matters.

I feel young, so I am young.

I am energized with the energy of youth.

My brain is strong, and I remember everything I want.

It's never late to start again.

Now is always the right time for anything I want.

TEA TIME #73

The day you decide to improve your self-talk is your lucky day. It's the first day of your most amazing life. It's the first day of greater things to come.

You're lucky, and you will feel lucky, because your life gets better and better. In fact, as things start lining up, life feels downright magical. *You are so lucky!* You get good parking spots. Green lights. Good deals. And if you don't get these every time, you don't care! You're too busy being happy!

I feel incredibly lucky to be living this stunningly fun life. I'm still in awe, years later, after changing the way I think. I'm the one who made it happen, and so can you. You do it by changing the words in your mind about everything.

You can do it. You... by showing up every day and changing any negative words and thoughts to positive ones.

I am lucky. So very, very lucky!

I live the luckiest life ever.

Luck is my jam. Luck is how I roll.

Luck finds me wherever I am.

I love being lucky!

I'm so grateful for how lucky I am.

I am worthy of luck!

TEA TIME #74

I fancy minimalism. Some people think the minimalism movement is for environmentalists or anti-consumers. I love minimalism because it makes my life simpler.

Less stuff. Less clutter. Less visual noise to occupy my brain. And less dusting!

It's an easy win for me. Simplicity makes my life feel more magical. When I have fewer clothes in my closet, I reserve energy from having fewer decisions to make—*gawd, what to wear?* This helps me make smarter decisions when it really counts.

Minimalism, for me, is freedom, and freedom is the core theme driving my life.

Where can you simplify and make your life easier?

Freedom bubbles up through me. My mind sets me free.

I appreciate simplicity, and it feels good to simplify.

I know my strengths, and I know how to shine.

I make great choices. I take time for me, to think and explore possibilities.

I show up to my life, and I pay attention.

My subconscious is powerful. I stand tall and strong.

I make great choices, and I feel good. I honor me.

TEA TIME #75

Language is the blood of the soul into which thoughts run and out of which they grow.

— Oliver Wendell Holmes

Your self-talk is just that... the language in the *blood of your soul*, and it determines that which *grows out of you*. Wow... so pick your words carefully. Intentionally. Choose optimistic words and thoughts so all the good things you want to grow will grow.

Before you master your inner dialogue, first you must be aware of it. This awareness is the very first step in living your most magical life.

Are you aware of the things you say and think? Are you self-monitoring your language?

I am amazing!

I own my language. I am keenly aware of my thoughts and words.

I am in charge of my thoughts, and my dream life follows.

I am rich with love and success.

The happy song in my soul beats stronger every day.

All is well. I am here. I honor life. I feel magnificent.

I'm patting myself on my own back. I show myself what I'm made of every day.

TEA TIME #76

If you're pushing, and trying, and squeezing your eyes shut real tight—*trying, trying, trying*—to live your magical life... and it's not happening... then you're going about it all wrong. You're trying too hard.

Trust me. It happened to me. (I admit, a few times. Ok, I *really* admit... quite a few times.) So, yeah, I've been there. I know when I'm headed in the wrong direction because I start making a thousand lists or drooling over spreadsheets. Or when I keep thinking through the same mental loop, and not getting anywhere.

When this happens, I know it's time to stop. To stop everything! It's time to smile. Better yet, to have a playful little smirk on my lips. Heh.

Yeah, it's time to chill. It's time to go outside and lay down on the grass. Or look at the stars. Or whistle a tune. It's time to forget everything except that I'm alive and breathing. That's when I start to notice more magic.

I am self-aware, and I know when to take my chill pill.

My life is expansive, and time is open.

I am comfy and confident. I am patient.

I love the pace of my life. I love smelling the roses on my journey.

Everything always works out well for me.

I am special. I am unique. I am a terrific person.

I am relaxed and calm, because I am.

TEA TIME #77

Have you ever taken a moment and officially welcomed magic into your life?

Did you ever send an invitation to your magical life, to let it know you're ready to party?

'Cuz when you do, the magic *will* show up. Magic loves a good party.

This kind of playful mindset can open the doors to your heart and mind. I know it seems silly, but seriously, you can't have a party if you don't invite people, or in this case, *magic*.

So, go ahead, invite magic into your life. Right now, with these words:

Magic, I welcome you into my life.

Magic, welcome, I'm here, waiting for you. We're gonna have a blast together!

Magic has RSVP'd to my party! It's coming! Oh wait, it's here!

Hi Magic, it's nice having you here. Thank you for coming.

I have a great relationship with magical living.

I love the magic I make in my life.

I am worthy of magic living in the party of my life.

TEA TIME #78

If a bomb is coming at you, it's coming at you. You can't go around worrying about it. Just go on doing what you love, and go on enjoying your life.

— MARK SULLIVAN, *BENEATH A SCARLET SKY*

I love this line from *Beneath a Scarlet Sky,* a novel about a boy in Italy during World War II. I read it about a year before I discovered my Coffee Self-Talk ritual. And I thought to myself, *isn't that so true?*

Things happen in your life. Stuff happens, sometimes beyond your control. Well, permission granted to go on enjoying life anyway.

Ya hear? *Enjoy your life anyway!*

The more I focus my brain on the good, the more good comes my way.

I give love to those in need, and my smile lights a path for them.

I am grateful for everything in my life, big or small.

I relax and enjoy myself, day in and day out.

Whatever happens, happens. I'm going to smile my way through.

I can change my mind anytime I want, for any reason at all.

I am worthy of joy and happiness.

TEA TIME #79

It was Dr. Joe Dispenza who implanted the idea in my mind:

You'll have your greatest success when you're most playful.

This made sense. Playfulness is an elevated emotion: it's lightness, it's goofy, it's fun. And you live your most magical life when you *feeeel* those juicy, elevated emotions. Hmmm... *if I play more, I'll attract more of the things I want.* I like this!

The problem was, I didn't know how to be more playful. I was too busy working, planning and ticking off to-dos. You know... working to make my dreams come true!

So I added lines to my self-talk about *playing.* I *imagined* dancing from the bedroom when I awoke. I visualized singing while the coffee brewed. I saw myself being silly with my family. And with repeated self-talk, the idea took root. I got comfy with it. I actually started playing more... And it worked! The days I play the most, I manifest the most.

I am playful and it brings magic into my life.

I am playful and it attracts abundance to me.

I am a magnet for greatness when I play.

I love playing through my day. It's my daily vitamin.

Playing, and dancing, and making goofy faces make manifesting easier.

I am worthy of a life full of playing.

The days I play the most, I manifest the most.

TEA TIME #80

Super weird is my happy place.

I know that I'm a strange duck with all my talk of magical living. When something falls and breaks, I laugh. When I go to my cafe and drink a coffee, I fall into gushing tears of gratitude. When I wake up in the morning, I laugh and dance.

When I stub my toe, I say *thank you*. When I have a headache, and I get an ibuprofen, and my mom says, "Oh, you have a headache?" I say, "Nope!"

Yeah, I'm super weird in these ways, and this super weird is my happy place.

Are you willing to be super weird with me? If it would make you one of the happiest people on the planet?

Come fly with me!

I laugh at life, and life laughs back with me.

If I make a mistake, I giggle and move on.

If my body isn't well, I infuse it with love and optimism.

When I wake up in the morning, I smile.

When I fall asleep at night, I smile.

All this minding of my mindset makes my life magical.

My mind stays elevated, and even if this seems super weird, it doesn't matter, because it makes me happy.

TEA TIME #81

If I say to you, *"Think back to yesterday, and remember all the great things that happened,"* your brain will start looking for the great things. It won't look for anything else.

But if I say to you, *"Think back to yesterday, and remember all the crappy things,"* you'll think of anything crappy that happened.

The difference in those statements is the word "great" or "crappy." See how a single word determines your entire focus?

What you see, and what you find, depend on what you tell your brain to focus on.

It's 100% up to you.

So be mindful of what you look for, and make it something that puts your heart and mind on the path toward magical living. This won't make all of your problems disappear, but some of them might. And others will shrink, becoming less important.

And it will make you much better at dealing with all of them, as you maintain a strong, positive, and forward-looking frame of mind.

I want the good, so I say the good, and then I see the good.

I choose better, and so I live better.

I changed my self-talk, and I changed my life.

Victory reigns inside me and my mind, at all times.

I am transformed. I am strong. My time is relaxed.

I rise. I rise. I rise. Every time.

I have integrity, genius, and patience.

TEA TIME #82

Flush!

Let's flush the seriousness of things down the toilet. Because that's what being overly serious usually is: waste. Why? Because making light of unpleasant things makes things easier to manage. It makes problems easier to solve. It makes life more fun. And happier.

I used to have so many rules. It was nutty! Rules about food. Rules about sleep. Rules about time. Rules about travel. Rules about dressing. *I was always so serious.* In fact, in my earlier days, a job interviewer once asked, *"What's your weakness, Kristen?"* I smugly declared, *"I have a hard time relaxing."* I wore it like a badge of honor. Well, over time, I paid the price... it took a toll on my sanity.

So much of what we think is serious actually isn't. It might seem important in the moment, but later it won't. Yet we get bent out of shape and waste time and energy with so much seriousness. Well, flush it. Save it *only* for the most critical times, like when a bear sticks his head in your tent.

I promise... when you flush the seriousness, you replace it with a more easy-going attitude. And this makes you happier and helps make your dreams come true!

I love being playful and laughing at life.

I have a deep ocean of peace inside me right now.

My life is lightness, that's my mode of operation.

I am love. I am light. I am grace. I am fun!

I honor my peace of mind.

I am worthy of light-hearted energy.

I find success easy with belief, love, and being silly.

TEA TIME #83

If I had a megaphone, I'd use it to blast this message to the world:

Problems are not the problem!

It's *how you see* problems that determines *everything*. One person sees trash. Another sees treasure. It's the same item, just viewed differently.

Every problem is a chance for growth. Yeah, sure, we want fewer problems, but guess what? You'll have far fewer problems when you live your magical life. That's how the magic works. First, you attract better things into your world. And second, for problems that do arise, you aren't fazed. Instead, you just get to work and take care of it.

Problems are not the problem. It's how you interpret the problem, with your opinions, beliefs, thoughts, and words (your self-talk), and how you go about handling them, with an upbeat attitude, looking for lessons and silver linings. That's the difference.

Do you have a problem right now that would benefit by looking at it differently?

My words and feelings determine my life. I choose awesome ones!

I deserve all the love that I want. I am worthy.

I deserve to love myself, as I am right here and right now.

I am excited to live my best life. I believe. Thank you.

I deserve all the happiness in the world. I deserve all the help that I want.

I deserve abundance and energy, and health, and joy.

I believe. Thank you. I believe. Thank you.

TEA TIME #84

When you use self-talk to manifest your dreams, you have a choice between thinking simple thoughts or detailed thoughts. When seeking a goal, consider including as many details as possible. For example, if you want to make more money, how much money? If you want a new car, what type of car? What color? The details help make a terrific mental picture for visualizing.

But wait! Simplicity also calls the magic! Consider this passage by Émile Coué:

> *People may wonder why I'm content to prescribe such a general —and apparently vague—formula as 'Every day, in every way, I'm getting better and better' for all and every ailment. The reason is, strange as it may seem, that our subconscious mind doesn't need the details. The general suggestion that everything 'in every way' is going well is quite sufficient to set up the procedure of persuasion, which will carry its effects to the different organs and improve every function.*

Go figure. If "short and sweet" does the trick, then kick butt and go for it. If you prefer buckets of glittery details, then by all means. Having both options available to you is powerful.

I am worthy.

I am a happy, fit, rockstar, worthy of the most rockin' life.

I am happy.

I am so happy I could skip, dance, jump, and run. All at once!

I am strong.

I am as strong as an ox, working the soil of my life, making magic!

I love my life.

TEA TIME #85

Right now. What do you think...?

Are you happy with your life?

Do you feel like your mindset is *magic*?

Are your days full of joy and laughter?

Do you believe your words impact your life?

How often do you smile?

How often do you complain?

Do you think you're successful? Why or why not?

Most successful people are not successful by accident. They *decided* to be successful. Happy people *decide* to be happy. It's a mindset. Is it yours? If not, it can be now. Have a mindset intervention. Just choose. Just say the words. Decide.

Repeat the words on the next page.

Believe in them.

Believe in you.

I choose success. I choose happiness. I choose love.

I decide my future by choosing my thoughts and words.

I believe in my success, because I've decided to.

My mindset is razzle-dazzle, because that's when I shine the brightest.

I decide to make my life what I want. I choose. I resolve. I determine.

I take action, today. I am triumphant.

I see the best. I feel the best. I live the best.

CONCLUSION & FREE BONUS

A Video Message from Me!

To watch a video message from me, point your phone's camera at this QR code:

Thank you for reading *Tea Time Self-Talk.* I loved sharing all these tips with you to help you live your most magical life. Keep showing up for your life, every day, and keep being awesome. And anytime you need a little boost of inspiration, flip open this book to a random page, and see what speaks to you.

I'd love to hear your story! Please write to me at:

Kristen@KristenHelmstetter.com

Or

Instagram: Instagram.com/coffeeselftalk

Podcast

Be sure to catch *Coffee Self-Talk with Kristen Helmstetter* wherever you listen to podcasts or at:

https://anchor.fm/kristen-helmstetter

Free Bonus PDF

If you'd like to receive a PDF with ten bonus Tea Times,

write to me, and be sure to ask for the "Tea Time Goodies":

Kristen@KristenHelmstetter.com

∾

I have a HUGE favor to ask of you.

If you would help me, I'd greatly appreciate it. If you enjoyed this book, I'd love it if you would leave a review for it on Amazon. Reviews are incredibly important for authors, and I'd be extremely grateful if you could write one!

∾

What's Next?

Here are more books in the Coffee Self-Talk family:

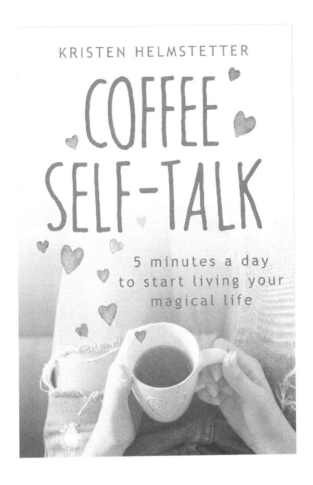

KRISTEN HELMSTETTER

COFFEE
SELF-TALK

5 minutes a day
to start living your
magical life

International Bestseller – Over 150,000 Copies Sold
Coffee Self-Talk: 5 Minutes a Day
to Start Living Your Magical Life

Coffee Self-Talk is a powerful, life-changing routine that takes only 5 minutes a day. Coffee Self-Talk transforms your life by boosting your self-esteem, filling you with happiness, and helping you attract the magical life you dream of living. *All this, with your next cup of coffee.*

The Coffee Self-Talk Starter Pages:
A Quick Daily Workbook to Jumpstart Your Coffee Self-Talk

It has never been easier to dive right into Coffee Self-Talk. This *Starter Pages* workbook takes you by the hand and makes it effortless to get started, with 21 fun, uplifting days of inspiration, affirmations, and simple, fill-in-the-blank exercises to jumpstart your daily Coffee Self-Talk ritual.

The Coffee Self-Talk Daily Reader #1:
Bite-Sized Nuggets of Magic to Add to Your Morning Ritual

This companion book offers short, daily reads for tips and inspiration. It does not replace your daily Coffee Self-Talk routine. Rather, it's meant to be used each day *after* you do your Coffee Self-Talk.

If you do one reading per day, it will take 30 days to complete.

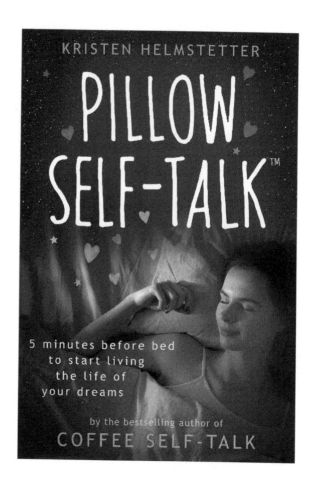

Pillow Self-Talk:
5 Minutes Before Bed to Start Living the Life of Your Dreams

End your day with a powerful nighttime ritual to help you manifest your dreams, reach your goals, find peace, relaxation, and happiness... all while getting the *best sleep ever!*

KRISTEN HELMSTETTER

WINE SELF-TALK™

15 minutes
to relax &
tap into
your inner
genius

by the bestselling author of

COFFEE SELF-TALK™

Wine Self-Talk:
15 Minutes to Relax & Tap Into Your Inner Genius

There is a source of sacred wisdom in you. *Wine Self-Talk* is a
simple, delicious ritual to help you relax, unwind, and tap
into your inner genius.

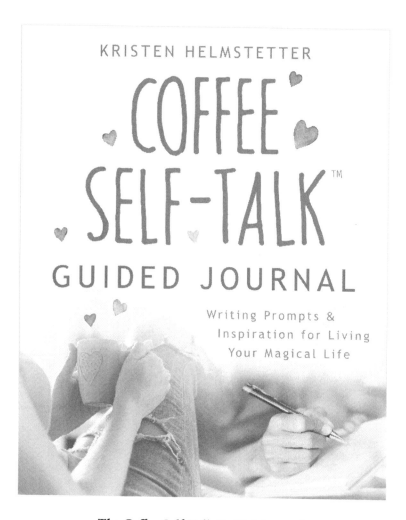

KRISTEN HELMSTETTER

COFFEE SELF-TALK ™

GUIDED JOURNAL

Writing Prompts &
Inspiration for Living
Your Magical Life

The Coffee Self-Talk Guided Journal:
Writing Prompts & Inspiration for Living Your Magical Life

This guided journal keeps you *lit up and glowing* as you go deeper into your magical Coffee Self-Talk journey. Experience the joy of journaling, mixed with fun exercises, and discover hidden gems about yourself. Get inspired, slash your anxiety, and unleash your amazing, badass self.

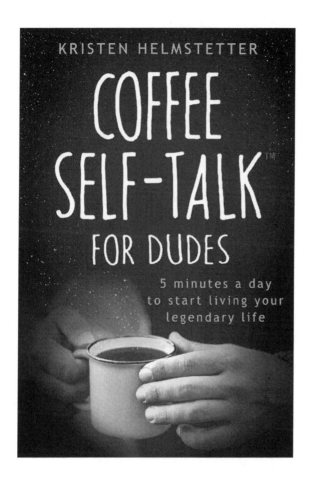

Coffee Self-Talk for Dudes:
5 Minutes a Day to Start Living Your Legendary Life

This is a special edition of *Coffee Self-Talk* that has been edited to be more oriented toward men in the language, examples, and scripts. It is 95% identical to the original *Coffee Self-Talk* book.

MY FAVORITE TEAS

Some of my favorite teas are:

- Andrew Lessman's Jasmine Green Tea
- Andrew Lessman's Earl Gray Green Tea
- Pique's Matcha Tea (ceremonial grade) and their other teas are great, too
- Blue Lotus Chai (black tea powder and spices)
- Numi Organic White Tea with Rosebuds
- Teapigs Black Tea (in the UK)
- PG Tips (in the UK)

I'm always looking for new teas to try! What are your favorites? Drop me an email at:

Kristen@KristenHelmstetter.com

Or ping me on Instagram: Coffeeselftalk

Made in the USA
Columbia, SC
30 August 2023

22305936R00111